BRIDGE TO NOWHERE

VICE AND VERSE IN THE CITY OF HATE

OLD MAIN PUBLISHING CO.
DALLAS
2016

Contents

Introduction

Dallas is my home. It is unlike any other place. But like any other place, Dallas exists completely *as it is*, filled with all kinds of hopes, problems, personalities, misconceptions, grains of truth, advantages, disadvantages, slummy burrows, shady characters, righteous works, delusional idiots, finger-pointing, tragedies, burger joints, and all the stuff in between.

If one is to go whole hog in loving a geopolitical construct, as I have chosen to do, one must acknowledge that every characteristic of that construct is true, from its morally murky history to its present reality. That does not mean, however, that one is required to accept these characteristics as intransigent arbiters of the status quo. In this country, one is allowed to speak up and effect change.

To say this city exists completely as it is, as I stated in the first paragraph, is actually a strong philosophical statement, one that may not be entirely true. You have to have people to make a city, don't you? Or would you consider post-apocalyptic Dallas with no population to still be a city if it's still got its skyline and signature empty trains? I don't know the answer, and this is where my logic breaks down.

I become even more embarrassed by my dwindling understanding when I think about each individual. What does one Dallasite think of another at any given moment? What does she think about the city? What does she think about the outsider? What does the outsider think about her? And what does the outsider think about her city? Now the notion of "city" is further convoluted and the inspiration for this book apparent.

Where do we go from here? I don't know about you, but I'm going to White Rock Coffee to get a blended mocha with no whip.

Sincerely,
c̲

P.S. I meant what I said about intransigent arbiters and speaking up and all that. Now, let's get to the poems.

For

Mrs. Fixler—my first and greatest encourager
I'm still working on that limo ride.

Dr. William Bedford Clark—without whom Whitman mumbles in the
pines
Princeton called; I told them you weren't going.

Bob—teacher, coach, boss, armchair philosopher, man after his own heart
Kino awakened in the near dark.

"Dallas is a second-rate city that wishes it were first-rate."

-Larry McMurtry

Dahl House

All is fair in Unfair Park
July 4, 2014
Between the porticoes,
Built in the Age of Orientals & Negroes.

We know what troubles the water,
Yet the people of the People's Republic of Dallas
Choose blankets over grass watching rockets blast.

All is fair in Unfair Park tonight;
All that divides us is the reflecting pool
Between the porticoes.

9:30 fire lights a star-spangled sky.
I'm eating a hot dog by a London friend
Who humours us for the night.

All is fair in Unfair Park tonight;
All of us does not all look alike.
We transpires beneath the porticoes.

Spain, France, Mexico,
Republic, Confederate, United, of an Art Deco mold—
Heil! Thy monuments to progress!

All is fair in Unfair Park
After 50 years 224 days,
Bound by attraction in the City of Hate.
Ain't that a Fair thing to celebrate?

Shadow of the Southwest

Does it begin in the wild grass
Scratching like a dog at suburban walls
Where pushy planned communities combat rural incursions?
Or under sturdy basement footings capping dirt and troglofauna?
Or high on building peaks at the kiss of steel and sky?
And where does it end when we see it only for Southfork or Olla Podrida,
Stevie Ray Vaughan in a different city,
Julius Schepps under his freeway, a juggler under a bridge,
Sol Dreyfuss and the Sangers, Jack Ruby in a bad mood,
Like Paris and its Eiffel, Rio and its Cristo,
Even if we could see it we could only perceive it, and that means
     everything.

Before He Dreamed

1955 was a Dallas amalgamation.
I met him in Titche-Goettinger while
He was running an errand for Mayor Thornton.
I made him late.
We married in five months. In Kansas.
Before he died last year,
He told me he never quit the job but
Got fired when he invited the mayor
To our wedding. My husband said he never regretted
Leaving the office that day to
"Meet the most unique girl in the store."

Vox et Praeterea Nihil

All of the renovation and city money in the world
Will not turn this neighborhood around.
Black folks here gotta drive to Frisco
For $30,000 a year,
And just think about the transportation expenses.
No, build a business, with fair paychecks,
Right here in town.
We need investors.
We don't need—oh shh shh
Willis Johnson is on . . .

Gone North

I was driving Dad to the airport
When I looked to the right and saw the prairies of my childhood
Overrun with the success of Valley Ranch.

Supply

I met a man in La Bajada.
He cried against the cinderblocks:
His boarded taquería.
I asked him why he cried.
The restaurants, he said.
The restaurants.
What about the restaurants?
We never thought, he sniffled and glowered,
We'd be competing against $10 potatoes.

A Bridge

Walk south on St. Paul and you will see
A real "Bridge" to nowhere
That the bums, who've always teetered on I-30,
Dart across and re-cross, day in and day out, like roaches over landfills,
Pinned between a thousand clones
Who will not hesitate to sell or steal a fix.

Crossed

Walk south on St. Paul and you will see
The Bridge
Crossed by hundreds on the way
To sobriety, ability, sanity, and independence.
You will see in their eyes the worst exhaustion.
They own no car, no home, no food, no family.
The vice grip of penniless exile
From a land of plenty to a land of plenty
Would stifle every future
Were it not for that Bridge to somewhere.

King Cotton

At Rosewood Mansion,
Lunch is served at noon,
And all the former farmers,
Ready to spend new money
With the Old Money,
Bring their lustrous wives
And gather in the dining room
For tea and chocolate truffles.
For the length of a meal,
Propriety tames the banks
Of a savage Turtle Creek,
When away in closets,
Behind the bespoken racks,
The wealthy men have stashed
An extra pair of boots
And a Smith & Wesson
Stockpiled for the day
When the veil of luxury,
Hospitality, and civility,
Thin as tissue paper,
Dissolves in Texas acid.

Anti-City

No city can evade the ugly truth
That urban stimuli
Stimulate derangement.
They named a bar after Oswald, after all.
Lee Harvey's. On Gould St. Check it out.
Few cities, however, can claim
To have been founded by the peerless
John Neely Bryan—
Indian Trader,
Trinity Ferrier—
Who shot a man in his lifetime
And laid the foundation
For the inevitable anti-city,
Just before coming home to roost
In Austin, where he was committed.

Suburban Legend

My friend from Philadelphia will convince you
That only plays, clubs, food, and music can give cities life.
I can tell you the exact night when Dallas came alive like never before,
And the only criterion was a bowling alley and the fated Lane 7.
We discovered, on a pitiful gutter ball, that a bump down the line
Would send the ball into flight, back over the wood, and knock down
The last pin for a spare. I tell you, the very ends of Dallas felt the bump
Was a city triumph and that the moment would never be repeated.
And it won't, because Jupiter Lanes closed down years ago.

Flash Point Mob

I went to the Boy Scout Hill restaurant presentation at LHBC.
And it started out like a joke:
An architect, a businessman, and 400 hippies walk into a Baptist church.
Naturally, chaos ensued and no restaurant was built,
So I wrote a letter to the Morning News (it went way over the word limit
       and I guess it was just too "real" for the editors to publish).
But my conclusion ran some ways like this:

      Some people turn vicious quickly
      For the love of the lake,
      Lake NIMBY.

Alls My Life

Oak Cliff raised me in the '90s
Crips baptized me at 16
But the only numbers that really mattered were
6'6'' 320
So I bareknuckle brawled in the streets
And broke ni**as to pieces
Until one day
I broke the wrong ni**a
And got baptized all over again

Backpacked

The kids on Katy Trail
Return from Copenhagen on Sunday,
Just missing church—darn it—
Holistically and totally vegan,
Except for, you know, wine and cheeses.
Non-negotiable.
And they will jog to keep healthy
And stop at the Ice House for suds
And rave about Rhineland gartens.
One must travel to fulfill his life, you see—
Variety the spice, say these wise vessels,
And when you jog,
Never veer from Katy Trail.

Mighty Trinity

Rage on, Mighty Trinity,
Handy Civic Divorcer,
Thrash thine haughty foes,
Devour all who trespass
And tread thy limpid depths,
As thou hast for centuries excelled.
For I have not wall to bar thee,
Nor bridge to cross thee,
Nor intellect to reduce thee
When rain and runoff swell thee.
But thou must soon beware
And fear the men who make Me,
Who grant My Being being,
Who own the very tools,
Strong enough to bend thee,
Of all thy power drain thee,
If only they could bridge themselves
And not before then wreck Me.

E.R.

D. handed over his keys and wallet and still was shot.
His mass is this morning at St. Pat's.
J. and a friend were killed in a car bound for Baton Rouge.
And my thoughts and concerns are with the family of D.H.
I pray the investigators find evidence of foul play.
Maybe these rains will put me to sleep.
Close thunder at 3 AM.

Home Visitors

It's funny.
We've lived in this city for 20 years,
And we've never been to this part of town.

Bliss

We talked about Little Rock.
We talked about Brown v. Board.
We talked about Rosa, Malcolm, and Martin.
We saw the dogs, the fire hoses, and the men in white hoods.
We saw the Stanley Forman photo—the strangest thing I have ever seen.
We even saw the lynch mob, proudly huddled at the feet.
But we did not discuss Dallas.
Did Dallas have a civil rights movement?
I know that Bobby Seale is from Dallas.
Did he leave to find the movement?
I do not think I know anything about my city.

"...the instability of a tall tower, a city's hunger for ruin."

Affordable Care

I shook Barack Obama's hand at Temple Emanu-El.
He smiled and I said thank you.
I owe him for my healthcare, something I have lived without for nine
     years
Until the exchange opened up.
I became a navigator to assist people like me with signup.
I wanted to tell him thank you a thousand times over
For what he had given me,
But I could not afford the reception at the lawyer's house.

On Glass Street

On Glass Street in the brick-and-mortar
1900s rust and rebar betray the age of a district we visit.
Like rafters cratering for new business, we are invited,
On a date, wandering into the mish-mash of art.
What a peach dress and winky giggling
At the silly Napoleons on stilts.
These bicorn-sporting French twins, one real, one trapped in a painting,
Bought into museo-conventions, which do not condone
Our disrespectful intentions to laugh at stilted Napoleons
Drawn by artists' coat-tucked hands.
Art does not a fun date make,
But humor can abolish that strange forever expressed in canvas,
Or in nails, toys, boxes, and songs,
Through physical manifestation or timeless inherence—
It will outlast us all, like my dream that night.
I saw an arrow-shaped garden sign protruding from mounds of sticks and
        smashed fruit,
Decayed and dripping off large marble pedestals.
I saw the sign and it saw me.
It pointed at Napoleon, then it pointed at me.
It pointed at you, then it pointed at me.
Forever, it said, forever.

Flu Shot

I took the bottle and drank and drove and killed
Four human beings at the hands of my money.
They call me Affluenza,
But my name is Ethan Couch.

"Hearts get broken in beautiful houses."

-Noel Jett

Sylvia and Nadine are not the best children.
But their mother sees how hard I try.
For three years—an alien in this place—
I did not understand their wealth.
I have come from poverty in places I do not remember—
Just the sand or the rain or the cold nights
Pacified in my brother's scarred cavities.
I saw his insides spilling from a swinging mace
And my papa stuffing them in before he lost his head.

In these thick, safe walls and clear glass,
Nighttime gaslights show books and special luxuries
We could not name in a dream.
I took Jealousy into my heart like a man into my bedroom,
And in the vast halls and under the big mantles
He paralyzed me and reminded me how much they have.
This household knows only fruit, He said to me,
Not the labor that bears it.
Their days are filled to the brim.

One garment in the wash I'd never seen
Flushed Jealousy out like a demon,
And the vast halls and big mantles grew larger,
The books withdrew into their shelves,
Madame spoke little and wandered ghostly
In the fifty percent she didn't want.
Sylvia and Nadine—not the best children—
Who will never worry about food or clothing,
Will understand their wealth in ways we cannot.

Un Naufrage au Texas

What was this place before we ruined it?
O indigenous and southerly Ozark,
Dinosaur bones clicking beneath the concrete,
Fighting to break through slabs of dissociated homes.
Where did this River venture, if not kindly to our feet,
Before we shut him up and banished him behind a dirt wall?
How did our verdant hills rise up and converse
And proclaim themselves the city's meccas,
And who were we, with flags and HOAs, to mount them?

10-Year Flood

This land is our land,
Notice how we conquered it.
O Tejas!
My friends, the Caddo, we thank you for it.
We, the Future, superseded *Tyrannosaurus history*,
Staved off the elements and fortune's flux,
Hid the surly water's remains in a ditch,
Mounted flag poles on hills.
May this tamed land serve its master well.

Friday Night

My helmet hung from broken hand,
My nostrils packed with blood,
The fans, the friends, the scoreboard cleared,
My sweetheart's knowing hug.
Life beyond, she claims, is sweeter,
What memories to come.
But some of me has died tonight
In football's solemn hum.
It ushers every freshmen in
And every senior out,
Ends seasons by time and inches,
Gives champions the rout.
So I, just I, alone at last,
In sacred turf shall kneel,
And say a prayer for all who come
To play on Texas field.
Though elsewhere boldly I may go,
And grow and die the same,
Linger here, my spirit, 'til
The final game is played.

Lights in the Eyes

He called it first and ten,
My recollection dims.
Trainers rushed the field,
But Bobby's fate was sealed.
I think about the mania,
That Friday night hysteria,
How far our voices carry.
To sports our moods are married.
If play is to live
What can living give?
Play took from me a son,
But thank the Lord we won.

World-Class

I am the Romans' woes—
Your city, my corpse, our big wreckage is gone.
We made little progress,
As progress was never put on the agenda.
A mix of warped morals and politics,
Business and interest, disinterest and divestment,
Washed up on the shores of Future City.
We were separate but equaled diversity.
Ancestral shame and shameful ancestors,
We bore it and our civilization we insulated,
Or we forgot them and bad myths we perpetuated.
From Future City to Fearful City, a city run on fear,
A city run by Cities within it,
That quashed the thoughtful voices,
Bleached the urban fabric, made it strange, elusive, sprawling,
And put words in our mouths that ended debates.
World-Class.

Martha's Boot

November 25, 2014
I pulled a rubber boot from a disturbed pond.
I pulled the foot out of it and took the boot home.
Down deep is Martha from the news.
And they would've seen her sinking
If blocking I-35 wasn't like clogging a jugular.
Sometimes, Dominique, if you just cut it, things flow.
Police were called to the wrong scene,
And I took a souvenir home.

Gentrifugal Force

When the people need artisanally popped corn,
They come to my Tyler-Davis shop and look no further.
Only the discerning dare enter.
I pop the corn myself and hand-coat each kernel
Whilst watching the city's bedraggled sheeple
Loaf aimlessly from Target to Walmart.
On occasion, quality will knock and taste will enter.
Tuesday's two customers dressed in fine rags;
They asked not about prices but farming sources
And decided on a pint of butter and scotch corn.
Two weeks later, these gentlemen returned with new appetites,
Which I sated in return for validation
And a good Yelp review.

Woman Found Beaten, Nude

Across from the Rugged Cross.
Malcolm X runs alongside Oakland Cemetery,
Home to barons, bosses, and belles,
And some acreage for all the rest.
As I walk the fence
I dab each iron spike with a finger,
Meaning to hit each one.
When I turn on McDermott I see nothing but growth,
Which is always the first symptom of decay.
Thick vines keel over a chain-link fence,
Fleeing the old, abandoned death within,
And then I notice the end of spikes.
So I turn back around, toward my apartment,
Dabbing the spikes like Monk.
I come to the park and, seeing the sign, laugh to myself.
"Opportunity Park."

Signifiers

I stroll through Lincoln Memorial on Sunday afternoons,
Wondering in the hot sun if anyone cares that this land exists,
Passing grave markers leaning adamantly in a direction,
As if to say,
"My body went that way. What're you doing here?"

DEARCY
CLAYTON
TEXAS
PVT
435 LABOR BN QMC
WORLD WAR I
SEPTEMBER 5
MARCH 23

On & On

Erykah Badu leased the Forest Theater for a few years,
Calling it the Black Forest Theater,
Referencing the demographics of South Dallas
And, more importantly, appealing to the neighborhood
For patronage and community support.
I guess the theater closed again because just the other day
I saw some tired men loitering around the green ruin,
Maybe waiting for a show that would never play.
Some famous names came through while it lasted.
I saw Dave Chapelle at the Forest before it went under.
And now I'm reminded of the old Chris Rock joke.
Remember his stand-up about MLK boulevards?
No wonder.

The City that Sleeps

You can hear the Zs in Dallas at night;
You'll hear nothing else in the City that Sleeps.
You'll pass through hollow steam and dead engines,
Hear the absence of footsteps and the crying mad;
They, too, find nooks in the dark concrete or ivy places.
No words are spoken on your drive in the streets
But the ones that Narcolepsy forms in your mind.
And you'll hear happenings over placid rails,
A dire ooze of paranormal appeal
Begging you to wake the city up.

Pepe's

Are you taking pictures?
You shouldn't take pictures 'cause the owners will get mad.
Are you cartel?
Are you cartel?
Hey, are you cartel?
You know what happened over there?
Cartels . . . [draws finger across throat] . . . right over there.
You shouldn't take pictures here.

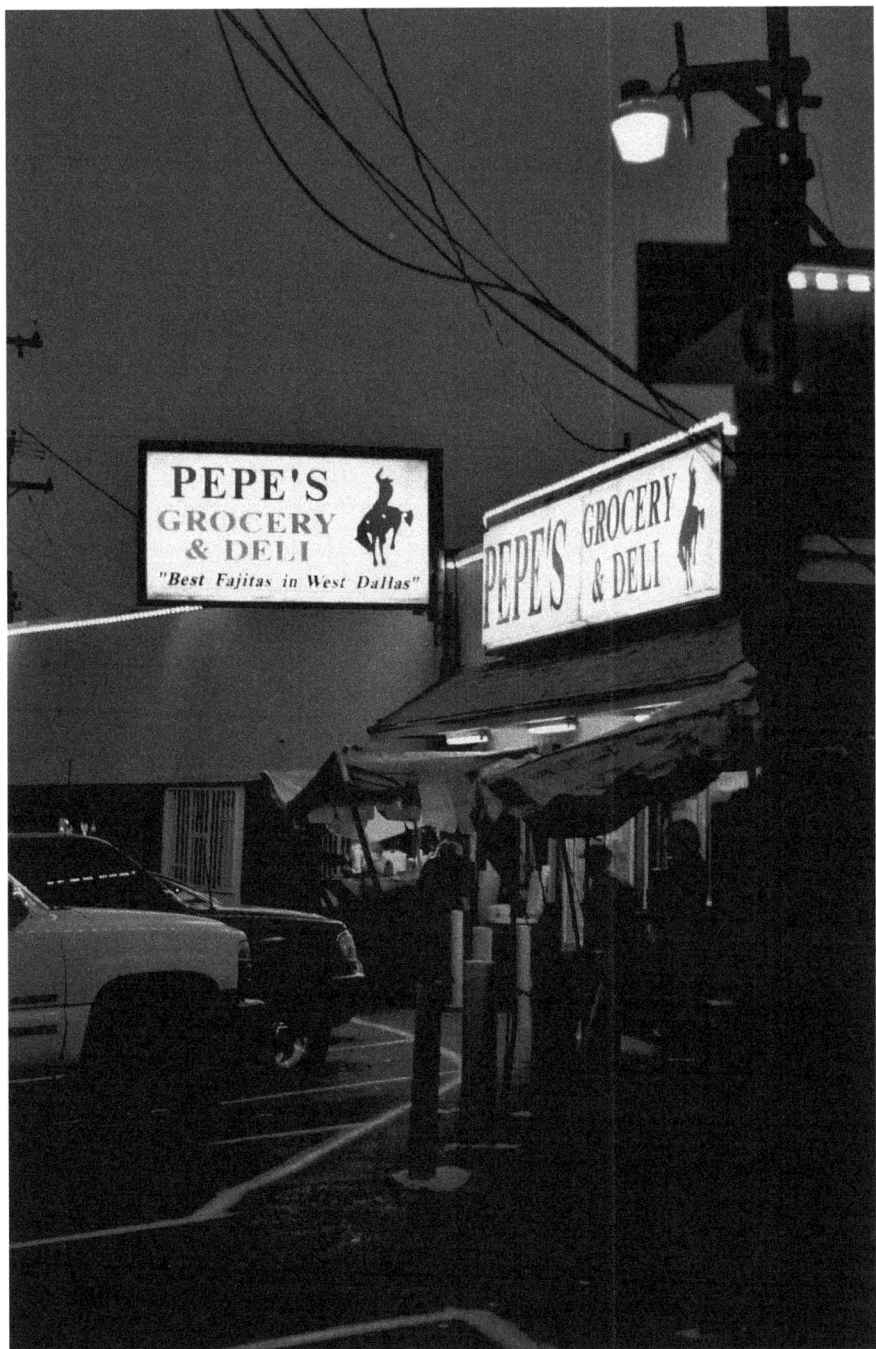

"The sign speaks till midnight."

Vox Omnia

From where will the new voices hail
If our soil isn't fertile?
I declare no land on Earth but ours can yield them.
I want no money for it. No plows. No hands.
Just give me room and a shred of conflict.
Give me the semblance of poverty and a Baltimore,
And they'll sprout by the hundreds and cry sharply out,
Desperate for the ears and hearts of another,
And you will know them as shade from a cloud,
The water you drink, the words you speak.
They will rise high and crush like tsunamis
And mix ruddy in the blacklands for aeons.

Poetry, Texas

I come from Poetry, Texas.
Say it right: *Portry*.
Dallas folk'd do well to heed it.
Talk day in an' out 'bout portry round a coffee cup,
But you'll never make it.
Ever been ropin'? brandin'?
Grown verse from the ground?
When's the last time you sat on a porch with the locust,
Lookin' out on a field and a dry river bed
And watched stars flare into existence?
You ever felt cracked board under your toes?
Held a woman tight and prayed
Right there for just one more day?
Ever hear a guitar snap that ancient, country quiet?
Or summer rains start tappin' metal sheds?
You can keep your city noise.
Leave the portry to us.

Buckeye Trail

I found an arrowhead off Buckeye Trail where
Nature, as it sometimes miraculously intends,
Had scorched the site with lightning bolts until the arrowhead
Stood on point in a clearing of scattered ash.
Sharper and more direct than at any state in its lifetime,
And dead to the ground,
I picked it up like a ticking bomb and threw it
Deeper into the woods
Before retaking my place on the trail.

A View from Little Mexico

I've lived in this town for 95 years and speak with authority.
I knew destined couples who died in each other's arms,
Parents who never saw their children die,
Bank accounts that never dried,
Minimum visits to a doctor,
Eighteen rounds of golf at Brook Hollow,
And successful affairs with receptionists—lots of those.
And I have seen just as many broken lives and families,
Broken bones and stabbings,
Beatings, slittings, castrations,
Bombings, displacements, humiliations,
Dumpster diving, garbage eating,
Starvation, dilapidation, third-world contraction
Of violence, poverty, injustice, and disregard. And worse,
I've seen alienation in a group of three
And wonder my place in three million and three,
This mild abuelita, who speaks with authority.

More Latin You Won't Understand

We look down on you from Mont-Saint-Jean—
French for Omni-Dallas-Hotel.
We're in bright lights, big city without you.
No crossing the Dallas Rubicon,
It's our own Maginot Line.
You know it as Interstate 30.
Socioeconomically, *alea iacta est.*

Audelia

You will know a rainy Dallas night
When you see red and yellow streetlights—
See them settle warped in black puddles
And scatter in the steam
Low-clinging to the pavement.
And your tires will depress at pothole edges
Just before you bound over them.
And the empty Audelia Road,
Tracing flat and straight the division of neighborhoods,
Will send you lonely down it.
And you will know a rainy Dallas night
As I have known them.

Grove Side Zeta

What must a Zeta think of a Dallas domain,
When his leader, 40, is arrested?
If he was stationed there to sell drugs or run guns,
And friendly surveillance is interrupted,
And all communication shut down,
Why not settle into a different kind of community?
A Zeta may decide one day to pick up the paper in a robe;
Wave at Mrs. Jiménez watering her plants;
Discuss One Hundred Years of Solitude in a book club.

He may read his Morning News with coffee;
Laugh at Steve Blow's timely, if intellectually stunted, Sunday column;
Roll eyes at Schutze's response.
Yearn for intimacy and marry a teacher at Comstock;
Raise a boy and take him to see the birds squawking in the Audubon
        Center;
Jump the creek with him in Pemberton Park.

If he picks up that paper,
Marries that woman,
Raises that child,
Will he live to be a man—a true and righteous Judas—
Unashamed to wash cars?
Or in his negligence be found
By Zetas, his earthly omegas,
And receive his traitorous due—
Falling headlong and bursting open in the street?

Fathom

He put them together with his hands—
The brass valves and the stainless bolts,
The copper pipes and the wooden deck—
And one morning in early winter,
Steered them, as one, through the channel.

When they sensed the open water,
They pounded and whistled
And threatened to break apart.
The captain scanned his gauges.
Finding nothing out of place,
He pressed on in measured calm,
Heading clean into fog.

They ferried him reluctantly into the black
Where he dropped the anchor and cleared their violent vigor.
He set them down in a drowning site.
"Here lie a city's dreams, unmarked by careless waves."
No other vessel, the captain thought,
Could take me to this vast solitude.
Only my steamboat
On White Rock Lake.

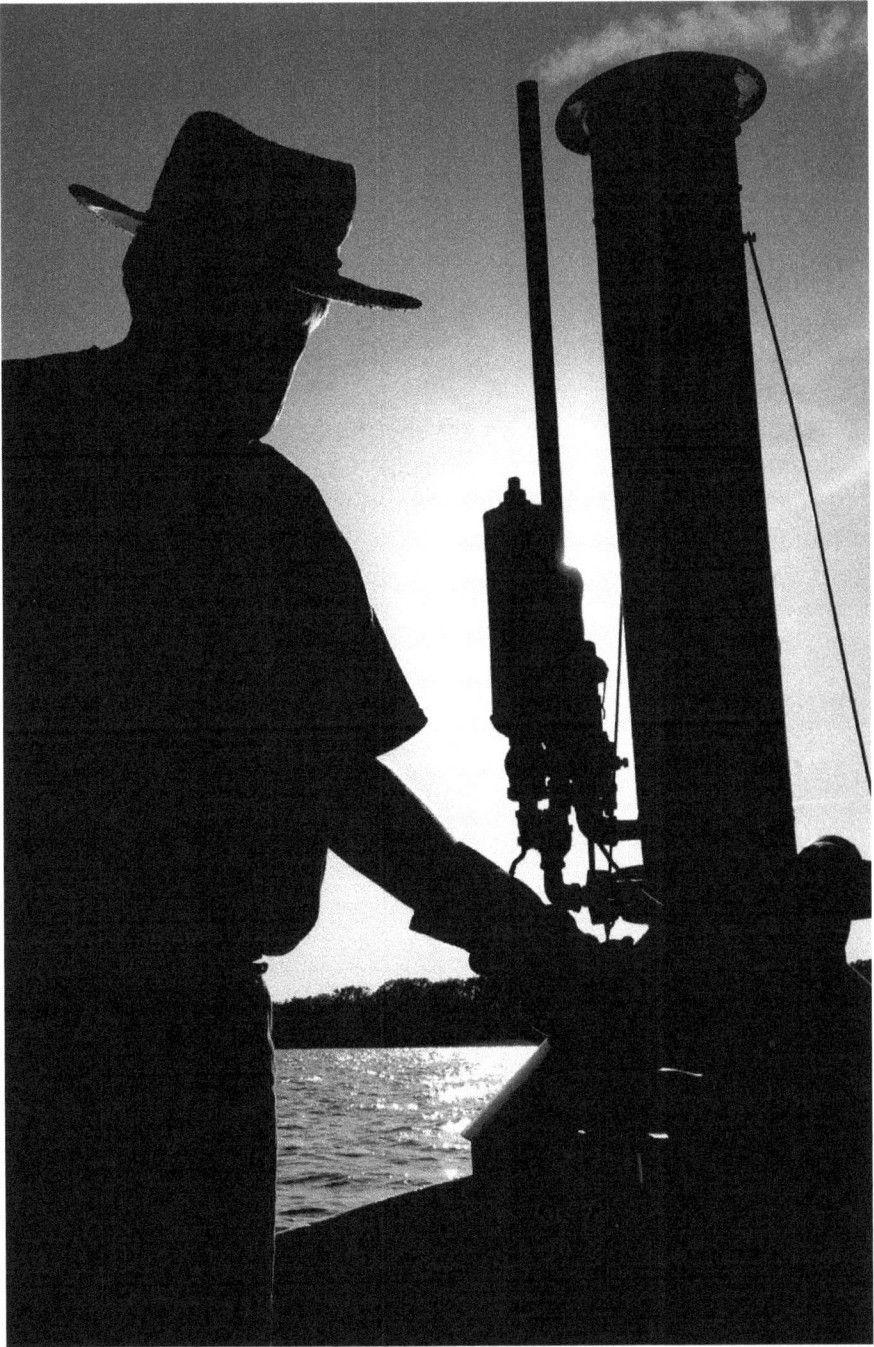

Morgan Fairchild

Morgan Fairchild lived in my neighborhood.
She was famous.
I didn't know for what,
But I imagined her a woman glowing brightly in a bathroom window,
Who never left her home, was never seen.
In my vision, she wore a pink nightgown in the house
And lounged with her cat on a white chaise, crying quietly,
Regretful she did not attend the block party.

First

With little support,
No cash on hand,
Few expectations,
And a shaken if not destroyed confidence,
I left home and went to college,
With a great SAT,
And brown skin,
And the odds of failure hanging over me.

CBD

You will not find old Dallas egos
Evinced in city towers.
They traipse, instead, the space between 'em,
Where affection flowers.

Calatrava

On my carcass they built their bridge,
Sewed two wastelands with a stitch.
Now mobile masses spring the ditch
And scratch that New York City itch.

Disunion

They reared Me like a Babel
In grand expanse, not height,
And would have splayed my limbs
From prairie to ocean,
If I'd lain but nearer the coast.

Denizens emigrated from my heart,
Little feeling the gut they stuck—
That hit below the belt,
That white-hot flight that sapped my lower extremities
With immoral capital evisceration.

And today, in this 21st century,
Our estranged brothers across the Mighty Trinity
Are left with broken culture—
Scared to death to lose it,
Unto death extol it.

Sympathy for the Devil

If I had killed Kennedy in 2014,
I would have fled north,
To the Park Cities.

Ticket

The Texas Theatre
Blade Runner: The Final Cut
09:00P 12/12/2014

Tabitha, Get Up

Is the FBI scared of corn rows?
That's an innocent man they took.
But when you're beloved by a few you're hated by many.
He threatened to take M16s to police cars,
He jammed a muzzle against an officer's head,
And all justified. Why? Because of the 80s and 90s.
Because of brutality. Police brutality. White brutality.
Young man, I know what you must think of me.
You must think I'm out of my mind.
But you've never heard a slave's voice, my great-granddaddy's voice,
One of Joppa's last, who spent his life in the field,
With his back under the whip and his head, as a rule, at the end of a
          muzzle.

Murder-Suicide

"The votes will be decided in the South. We always do."

John Wiley Price

"I promise I will not be obedient without the use of chains."

Give me color and a seat at the table,
And I will promise you anything.
Give me your vote, give me your trust,
And I will protect your way of life
If it means denying every rich white man—
Who dares invest in you—
A stake in your worth.
You don't need a dirty business
When you've got a man downtown.
Give me your confidence,
For I am my brother's keeper,
And when opportunities arise, you can bet,
I'll always take advantage.

The Father

Yeah I banged with Fishtrap Bloods for a bit
Back in the summer, I don't know, '94?
They taught me reputation, how to intimidate.
I learned boundaries, where you went, where you didn't.
I got something I couldn't get at home,
I mean, these guys were proud of me,
They respected me.
Mattafact, my Daddy did me a favor. Mom too.
So I ain't worried.
My boy'll be ok, if he finds the family
I found in the streets.
Yeah yeah I'll call you tomorrow same time
If they let me.

The Sin

I listened to John Denver while jogging Five Mile Creek
And suddenly couldn't believe I was jogging in Texas at all.
An endless line of trees annulled my Dallas image,
And nature's unraveling path before me
Got me believing I'd awoken in West Virginia,
Fresh from Lynchburg to this promised land.
Resting Free, here in the mountains,
I witnessed the iconoclasm of institutional violence,
For a moment,
Before I stopped at a gas station to get water
And took my bullet behind the ear.

Self-Assertive Manhood

My father, by his actions, taught me how to give.
He could barely afford the mortgage on our house,
But he was always willing to serve the vagrant folks
Who stumbled onto 51st Street in nothing short of a regal stupor.
Attracted by our checkered garage, they drug knuckles down the front
      door
To say hello to no one in particular,
And with his valuable time and resources, my father
Lent them coats in winter, hats in summer,
And drove them home or to a shelter.
I, myself, have stumbled and knocked,
But Dad's no longer there to answer.

Trampoline

My parents bought me a trampoline in 1983,
The best that year had to offer,
And I had friends over everyday
Begging to jump on it, but I wouldn't let 'em.
Peaking just over the trees on Willomet Avenue,
Over Oak Cliff's actual cliff, only I
Met the skyline on an up-bounce,
While my friends down below yelled at me for hogging the trampoline.
But they didn't know about the view above, the view of Downtown.
They didn't know about my dreams of going there one day
And becoming a real Dallasite.

Descent

When they finally caught me leaving Red Bird Mall
And asked me why I'd shot the man
In the neck for his phone,
I said as plain as I'm saying to you now,
"I didn't need the phone.
I just needed to prove to myself, once and for all,
That I was a real Dallasite."

Rock Bottom

I passed a figure on Commerce
Processing reverently, as a priest,
Hunched beneath a dirty cloak
And dragging his crusted feet.
He turned suddenly into an alley
Where he hid for the afternoon.
By 3 o'clock I'd joined him
In his cardboard saloon.
The spread was ready,
Glass to the moon,
"To tailored ambition!
You took us too soon!"

Sunbelt

I left my person at home and went walking downtown.
I passed parking meters and stoplights.
A homeless man napped on a bench.
Birds leapt from the sidewalk as I approached.
Restaurant owners tidied up for evening business.
Suits trickled out of revolving doors.
An officer, shaking his head, drafted a ticket on his pad.
A bus full of commuters stirred up a cloud of dust and newspaper.
Skyscraper windows refracted the orange sunset.
Night came and music played and thoughts weighed,
How unfortunate our city resembles every city laid.

Convert

The train whisked us over paths and creeks
And ushered us into the city's heart
Where men and women, larger than life itself,
Trounce the very walks they pave
And call time on the workday they schedule.
We clamored in the shadows of thespians
And played darts in bars with governors.
Lovers entreated; no lovers relented.
Cops of all kinds tipped hats and proceeded.
We crossed the street in purple sunset,
In music my soul had never acquainted,
No city like this city, New City, created.

Herschel Renner

Herschel Renner moved to Dallas from Minneapolis, MN.
In early January he caught the trolley to Big Al's bar.
Soaking in the kind of unwinterly warmth he'd never known,
He informed me of the sites over my liquor.
Dallas! *L'essence de la modernité*!
The Winspear and "The Eye."
How big, he raved, Big D could be.
(I did not know any Herschels until this exchange
And longed never to know one again.)
So, when he concluded his commendation,
I, cleared to go home to Bonton,
Said to him, "Sit. Please sit.
Drink until you've sobered."

East Dallas Alternative Hedonist Society

They took me to a brown brick house in the forest plastered with signs that
      gave me the sudden urge to drive as though my kids lived there.
I kept my eyes wide shut while their brutal bestial bodily instruments
      negotiated the natural.
Kings and Queens, Philosophers and Physicians (Plato and Dr. Watson
      themselves!), or Writers and Mothers stayed awhile—the homeless
      living in endless house.
Guy and Edna Ballard, Ascended Masters, descended for an evening.
They served mixed drinks and creatures from local habitats, like toads,
      cockroaches, and geese.
They sniffed the entrees, every last one of them, delighted in the
      fragrance, then ate nothing.
When schools and general communal living were broached, they went on
      impertinently about the French and wiped clean hands with the
      Stars and Bars.
They read my mind and rebutted, "No *you* are the peculiar one!"
They danced while sitting.
After all, were they not doing their part correctly, as Mme. Sosostris
      assured them?
And I imagined that no descendant of mankind could say these people had
      not lived and fashioned their own out of so many breaths.
So I said goodbye and got out of Lakewood as quickly as I could.

But their Preston Hollow kinfolk snatched me up;
Boxed and shipped me to pleasant Koon Kreek Klub.

Mx. Dallas

Clean and gritty succubus,
Rained and shone upon,
Killer and birther,
Builder destroyer,
Rapist redeemer,
Hot and bitter incubus,
Hermetic asexual city,
Green and grimily
Limitless in humble ostentation

"Like any small town...

...Puamahara has its factions, frictions, fictions and fractions.''

Moving Product

Four clients and I lounged lucid in the woods,
My pockets full, soon with cash,
When nine missionaries crawled through poison oak to talk.
They spoke to my clients softly, pitching and pitching,
While I steamed within—that competitive spirit.
We battled in the commune,
They for the hearts,
I for the minds.
We will see, when these missionaries leave,
Whose product lifts more souls.

Pies on Gladiolus

Miss J. called me in from the people I hung with.
We baked a pie together.
She flattened the crust by hand and I filled it with apples.
She said half was for my sister.
Dad was in his alley.
Just a secret between us girls.
Now that I'm a woman
I've learned to bake pies
And would gladly share one with you.

Reluctant Ambassador

Visitors will ask,
"What's there to do in Dallas?"

A proud resident
And reluctant ambassador like myself
Fears misdirecting them
And letting down the city.

Truthfully,
I don't have the taste for "things to do,"
But prefer the shade under my red oak
And the twiddle of sparrows
Nesting in the eaves.
That is Dallas, to me.

Eighth Wonder

My feet rose from the pavement
As I, a weary traveler, approached the twilit monolith.
Like a moth to a spotlight,
The glory drew me near.
I knew at once the rapturous upheaval,
The dying man's esoteric knowledge,
As I ascended to the starry opal of the night.
Fanfare burst forth from the bright canopy,
Resounding in the Middle City,
Rattling the ramparts of this silver celestial
Whose very sighting scuttles reason,
Drags the salaried from their dirty slums,
Makes believers out of skeptics,
And blinds those who see the end—
Dazedly wrapped in glass and a retractable roof.
No longer must I keep up with them,
For Mr. Jones himself has bridged that gap for me,
Asking nothing more than loyalty
And a month's rent to see the Boys play on Sunday.

Ebola

There is a reason Ebola came to Dallas.
There is a reason Saturday Night Live,
In all its Lampooning,
Could not understand the connection
Between Dallas and the African continent.
Or the difference between the continent and its countries.
Or the difference between Dallas and Texas.
Or the difference between Texas and "Texas."

Our New England comrade,
Our Big Apple affiliate,
Our nation's signature pot in which many people stew,
Cannot conceive a land as worldly as it,
That hosts the tempest-tossed without fervent rejection,
And draws him not dissimilarly into 20th century stagnation.

Reuse, Reduce, Recycle

Krall Place, unmarked road
(1/2 mile south of Strevell, turn at old replica wikiups)
Standrod, Idaho-side 83342
Inquire with postmaster

Dear Mom,

Email would have been easier, but I wanted to tell you
I've found a home. State-Thomas.
We've got everything here in this old part of town.
Old, but it feels so young.
I do as the residents do.
We walk and talk by day and night.
We eat produce under maturing trees.
We converse but don't seem to bother one another.
If you've got a dog you walk him near the rock wall,
Near the base that holds tall iron bars in place to keep Greenwood out.
That's the cemetery. It's the neighborhood's history of people.
People who didn't look a thing like you or me
Have been buried behind the wall, or maybe only some have.
Maybe their burial parcels were confiscated, too,
But at all hours I hear them speak and smell their incense
Rising over the wall and trickling into the streets.
Bitter, suckered moaning is blasted and laid with State-Thomas bricks.
I'm sure of it.
In this newfound home, I live with the whispers.

I sure love my city, not sure if my city loves me.

Cain,
With love

Human Sacrifice

When I hear the detritus spigots
Excoriate the Shadow City's champions,
Call them tasteless, puffed up, insecure,
And in turn absorb the parry—
An always polished recitation
Of the Man-Made City's many triumphs—
I think of the seventeen children who,
After a proper beating and a merciful death,
Likely cared very little
For this town's aspirations.

Prairie Town

When they see your face and hiss and miss your bubbling heart,
Mistake stars in your eyes for cataracts,
Laugh when you stumble and claw for their esteem and station,
Bury your successes under a mountain of history,
List your candor under the excesses of youth,
Just know they feared you
When you were fearless.

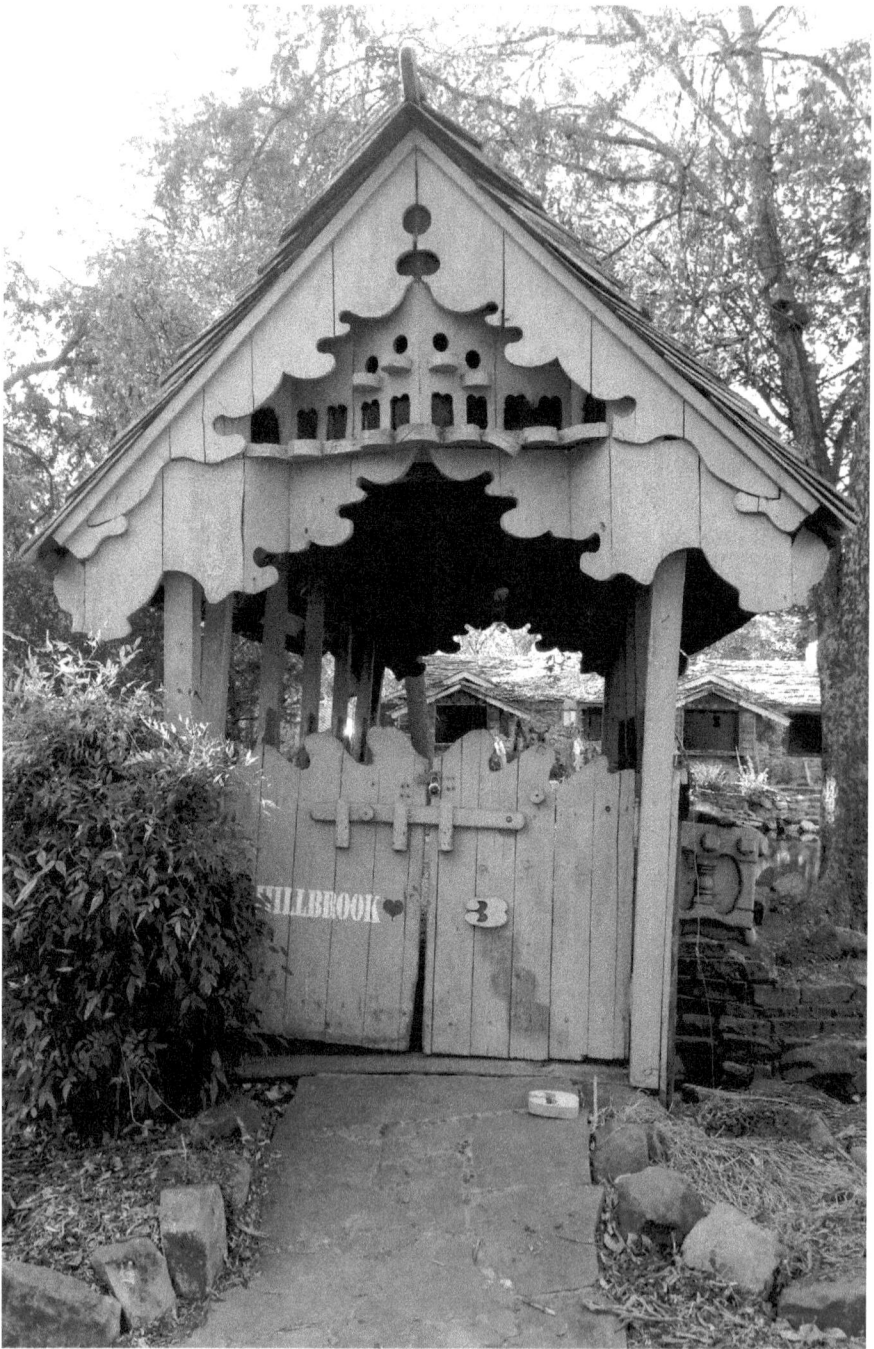

To Infinity

Fear nothing here,
We will progress
At a blinding pace.
Have only I the taste
For history as it dictates
Our current state?
Future's drum is beating,
That exponential bleating;
There is no time.
There is no time.

DFW

Dallas will always hear the good news.
The land of perpetual economic growth.
People will always come to stay.
We'll always be proud of our talent.
Just as long as we call Dallas by another name.

The New Old Parkland

I delivered five cheese pizzas to Old Parkland.
At first they wouldn't let me in.
But some children ran to the gates and pushed away a senator's aide.
Thank you for the pizza, ma'am, you can keep your change.

Nowhere

On my side of the bridge, tolls are paid in perception and, eventually,
Cultural asset forfeiture when artsy bottom-dwellers set up shop
And the masses packed with Benjamins catch wind of the grungy,
Compelling happenings that no exec could conceive. So he
Purchases the quaint town of Nowhere and takes his loot across
Our bridge and trades our neighborhoods for booths to toll our kids.

1500 Marilla

Out of the asphalt fissures,
Where the citizens transport,
Out of the mufflers soaring through sensors,
Out of the shallow pockets and into the deep,
Out of vain, propitious, gargantuan investments,
Construction delays to the point of no returns,
From the bleeding hands that hold the real stake,
Out of the mouths of forward-thinkers
Always thinking backwards,
Near the all but stationary cogs of disorder
Creaking into motion,
Out of gritted teeth and collapsing shoulders,
Out of dormant distrust between Dallasites,
Where and how the people live,
Where and how they work,
Old murmurs violate the air
Spinning webs of forgotten greed.
Candlelit notions shine on the voices,
Muttering…
Tammany Tammany Tammany

Centennial

Fair Park in the early morning—no one knows *I* am here.
I enter in a fog on the esplanade that envelops and retards my gait.
I press on, into the porticoes.
I pass the brawny mural figures, content to work forever.
Though they be in me, 'tis I them, and they disapprove my trespass.
They toil loudly and make angry progress as I cower into the mist.
Ciampaglia's commotion degrades in the distance; a golden archer looks
   for his arrow.
I take refuge at the jolly boots of Big Tex, finding naught but the ash of
   incinerated fabric falling on a stubborn frame.
I spy an ancient woman, Spirit of the Centennial, pacing in skeletal
   shadows.
She wails and curses "this petrous grin!" for so much weighs on her heart.
After all, in 1845, she voluntarily surrendered her sovereignty.
I take her pale marble hand and lead her down the bleak paths.
We come upon the barns and pavilions stocked with inanimate animals
   lying frozen in the dirt.
We circle the Cotton Bowl, a sportless sanctum and former redoubt.
Athlete nonexistent, locked gates cannot contain the black humour roiling
   within.
Midway shudders in a muted pollution of no bodies risking the empty
   stalls.
The Ferris wheel's zenith vanishes in the fog.
The lagoon and its lily pads repel us.
Meanwhile, the Hall of State lies timorously in a far, feeble shroud—
This Westminster Abbey of the New World bunkered by the suzerain
   Luftwaffe—
Internal fascia fastened by the rhetoric of in-power and empowered anti-
   yet ante-fascists.
They just don't know it yet.

His dementia rehearses for lynchings; his wheezing haunts our footsteps
and echoes in the past.
He pleads for CPR under six flags reading, "Please Resuscitate," so Lady
Centennial draws away to comfort him, unsure how to resuscitate.
I am left a static clinging at the nexus of American reality, where things
are black and white, akin to Tolson's Rhapsody, to ask my fellow
cities, then:
Why does my Fair morning die dyed in funny sunshine?
In a jaded complacence of 20th century stagnation?
No science in the Science Place?
They still do music in the Music Hall?
Why have we stopped reaching?
Have we reached too far, not far enough, or wandered into the pall?

. . . in the dimension of life that is beneath and beyond literal truth, in the spiritual world where willpower and ideas and emotion and accident invent the bones of reality, the Dallas myth is a reflection of fundamental and absolute truth. All of the dust-caked, flinty-eyed farmers who came down into Texas in the 19th century made towns, and most of those towns are dead and dying today. But Dallas is a great city, clearly destined to become one of the great cities of the next century, and all of that is due in some important part to the work of the people who live and have lived there. People in Dallas can do something people in Paris cannot do. They can look at their vast gleaming city and know, just as surely as they know that the sun is hot and water is sweet, that it is they who made the city, that it would not be there were it not for what they do and have done. It is a city whose glass slab towers are made of human dreams and whose streets are paved with human grit. -The Accommodation

The End

About the Author

For information, contact the author at 2linesunderc@gmail.com

www.ingramcontent.com/pod-product-compliance
Lightning Source LLC
Chambersburg PA
CBHW061148040426
42445CB00013B/1616